3 Weeks' Notice

Amy Pattison

Presentation by *BookLeaf Publishing*

Web: www.bookleafpub.com

E-mail: info@bookleafpub.com

ISBN: 9789357212267

First edition 2023

To me. For managing to maintain a habit for 21 days. And you, for reading this rather unorthodox and anachronistic anthology.

Idiosyncrasies

Planning out the day on the day before,
Minute by minute, hour by hour,
From waking up, up to starting to snore,
Every detail, each half hour shower.
Using the radio, watching TV,
Think about the noise every single time,
Make sure the sound is a power of three,
A palindrome, times by five or a prime.
If an event is meant to start at noon,
Five minute drive, but take ten for traffic,
Double Google Maps' time and get there soon,
"Waiting in the car," a biographic.
Multiple things which put me ill at ease,
These are a few idiosyncrasies.

Over and Over

It's happened again.
I told you forever ago,
I love you like the night sky - sometimes the
best parts are hard to see.
But behind the ceiling, the clouds, and the
distance,
Sparkling just for me is you.
And if I wait and stand by you, keep looking up
to you, a shooting star,
(I already have my wish).

It's happened again.
I told you the other day,
I love you like the colour red - bleeding into all
of my life, a heart on fire.
And in those flames are the blazing memories,
Thawing me, warming me, burning me.
No matter the degree, celsius or burn, you're
worth every scorch mark,
(Everything smells like smoke).

It's happened again.
I'm telling you now,
I love you like a story - happy endings and plot
holes. Victories and betrayal.

Reading between the lines, I saw a thousand
words,
A white knight mounting an ignoble steed.
And the credits roll as you ride off into the
sunset,
(I'm starring in the sequel).

It's happened again.
I'll tell you soon,
I love you like a storm - electric and electrifying
and always gone too soon.
Lighting up my world in flashes, I blink. I miss
you,
The dark seems darker without you.
Blinding when you shatter my world, I would
stay broken for you,
(I think I already am).

It's happened again.
I'll tell you one day,
I love you like an explosion - drama and
screaming and nothing will be the same.
How can you fix a life in pieces?
You can't.
You build.
But what's a building with no foundation?
There's gaps in the walls, holes in the roof, I
don't have a chimney,
(Time heals burns too).

It's happened again.
You'll never know,
I love you like a dream - I don't remember my
dreams. But I'm smiling when I wake.
Stretching my limbs and cracking my back,
yawning through my hand,
Somehow, the sun's rising without you.
Putting the pieces back together, the day starts
anew once more,
(I'll fall in love with you).

Impossible Things

Why is a raven like a writing desk?
Is there another word for thesaurus?
When you add one, is infinity more?
A dinosaur - do you think he saw us?
Can you remember tomorrow's tonights?
Or make an unstoppable object stop?
Hear the sound of silence as it rises?
Or dance fantastically with a mop?
What is the opposite of opposite?
If it is so cheap, then why do we talk?
What are we, but a collection of thought?
If a tree grows two more feet can it walk?
Who is the person trapped in the mirror?
Can you know what it is that you don't know?
If it is untravelled, is it a road?
When not here, where do all the lost socks go?
If nothing heard it, was there really sound?
If the end's not the start, was it a quest?
Can questions be truly impossible?
Why is a raven like a writing desk?

Haiku

6

A little poem
A beat of five, next seven
Then five syllables

When I Grow Up

I thought maybe I'd be an astronaut,
A scientist or a mathematician,
That I would be witty and provoke thought,
And sideline as an awesome magician.

I thought I'd be skinny and glamorous,
A model, a poet, or an actress,
A popstar and not part of the chorus,
And that I would be fun, fab and famous.

I thought I'd be a renowned genius,
That I could answer any question posed,
What I'd say would be taken serious,
That I could just breeze through life unopposed.

I thought lots of things about growing up,
Good thing there's still time before I'm grown
up.

Fate

A web of opportunities for you,
Catching you when intentions go awry,
A security blanket you can't view,
A reason when your friend is the bad guy,
When the job you applied to rejects you,
When it didn't work out on the first try.

But if predestined, is there ever choice,
Why put in effort if the book's been read,
Is it ever our win, should we rejoice,
Or do you think we're a puppet on thread,
Are we just speaking with another's voice,
What if we want to say more than was said?

Maybe it's not a war that can be won,
Why fight the ending if the answer's great,
Does that lack of freedom make it less fun,
When you get to start dating your soul mate,
Or get to spend summer days in the sun,
Maybe it's not wrong, that we can't fight fate.

Where Wolves?

A night like any night, quiet and calm,
Nothing to say you'd come to any harm,
Nothing out of place, no cause for alarm,
The kind of night that would leave you
disarmed.

Dreary clouds making way for a full moon,
The dark feels like it's going to consume,
But you walked this route just this afternoon,
Don't rush to Grandmother's, you'll get there
soon.

A cold breeze fights to push back your white
hood,
Shivers trace lines down your spine where you're
stood,
In the deepest, darkest part of the wood,
Which starts to feel like it might not be good.

Red eyes slowly emerging from the dark,
Bringing a putrid stench to the warped park,
With teeth that could rival sharks they're so
sharp,
Against its dark matted fur, they're so stark.

Quickening your pace and not looking back,
Head down, hood up, and stay on the right track,
They may be there, but you're hidden in black,
If you can't see them, then they can't attack.

A foolish hope, you should've ran instead,
When you started to feel that sense of dread,
Now it's far too late, because out you've bled,
The once white hood now stained a scarlet red.

Breaking News

Every minute, more notifications,
A player kicks a football in Qatar,
It's being played on all TV stations,
Not so bad, but I find the game bizarre.

Train strikes seemingly every other day,
Coincidently when I need them most,
Rescheduling, finding another way,
If I meet the one in charge, they'll be toast.

The cost of living's having a crisis,
I think I know exactly how it feels,
All I've ever bought's rising in prices,
It shouldn't cost this much to cook my meals.

Ice caps are melting, sea levels rising,
Coral reef bleaching, polar bears dying,
Paper straws, from government advising,
Large corporations fossil fuel buying.

Iranian women burning hijabs,
Cutting hair and fighting "morality,"
Iran authorities watch and keep tabs,
With misogynistic brutality.

The news app on my phone is incessant,
On insta all I can do is doomscroll,
Maybe I'll try TikTok, less depressant,
Find a way out of this painful black hole.

Remembrance Day

On eleven of eleven at eleven A.M.,
Bow your head in silence, let the quiet spread.
Two minutes we take, one day every year,
To close our eyes and feel their fear.
Wear a red poppy to show your belief,
They shouldn't have died, on their graves a
wreath.
Every year 'tis a day of elevens,
Thousands of soldiers rose to the heavens.
Till November eleventh, nineteen eighteen,
When guns fell silent, 'twas the end of the scene.
Four years it took for the fighting to stop,
Wooden crosses upon the dead atop.
So many deaths that we try to remember,
The ones occurring up till November.
They fought for their country and died for it too,
Sacrifices made, for me and for you.
Though it went to remembrance from armistace,
The catalyst being a world war twice.
We remember all those who gave their lives,
For the day of elevens, through time survives.
So many days, before November,
So many days, and yet we remember.

Travelling

It's not great when you can travel for weeks
Needing only the bags under your eyes
Eyelids falling closed of their own accord
Pinching yourself to give you a surprise

Face feels puffy and eyes a bit bloodshot
No time to fix it, no super powers
Snoozed through my alarm, but it's not my fault
After I slept, it gave me five hours

But don't worry, I'm a dab hand by now
A coffee (or two) a day, maybe more
Sing in the car so there's no time to think
Stay on the go and you won't start to snore

Lying in bed and it's well past midnight
Just put the phone down, it's not difficult
You can't seem to focus anyway now
Tonight's the night to try something different

Five hours later, we rinse and repeat
Approaching the night with trepidation
Knowing the morning will come far too soon
That's how life goes with sleep deprivation

Brunch

Brunch is better than lunch or than breakfast,
It's the perfect place for merrymaking,
And it's at the best time to break your fast,
No-one wants full meals just after waking.
You can order a mimosa or tea,
A bloody Mary or cappuccinos,
No other meal has such variety,
From ordering sweets to jalapeños.
Brunch is also better than dinner too,
Don't have to go to bed too soon after,
Time means you've the whole day ahead of you,
A day full of friends, good times and laughter.
Brunch is better than lunch, breakfast, dinner,
Think otherwise? You're just a beginner.

Christmas

Decorating the tree with mum today,
Advent has started, it's first December,
So we can get excited this Thursday,
Christmas build up starts after November.

Drinking mulled wine, having fun by barrels,
German markets and then online shopping,
Listening to Christmas songs and carols,
Once the spirit grips you, there's no stopping.

There's presents on the special day itself,
Crackers, bicycles and clever toy planes,
But the best gift you can bring is yourself,
For a frosty walk down cold and crisp lanes.

A chocolate a day, keeps krampus away,
The wine gets better with every toast,
Food's better at a family party,
And there's no roast like a Christmas day roast.

Food + Me

The caramel nibbles are finished by the time I
get home.
I feel sick at the three quarter mark, but push
through.
Lying on my bed later, feeling awful and
regretting it,
I order more, saying it's the last time. That's not
true.

Feeling full but I'll stop after I've finished this
packet.
Even then, on the lookout for a chance to binge.
Many failed plans where the only thing I lose is
my mind,
Looking back at some of my diets makes me
cringe.

Running on the spot when a Wii game calls me
obese.
Weight loss shakes, detox drinks, and diet pills,
What will it take for food and I to be at peace?
How much more can my body take before this
kills?

Exercising to punish myself for having to eat
lunch,
Maybe I will end up the size of a bus after all.
If one more person says they think I've lost
weight,
I'm going to break apart and crawl into a ball.

End of the year, you'll never guess my
resolution.
No really, I'm trying something different this
time.
No scales, counting calories or avoiding the
mirror.
I'm going to focus on something that lasts a
lifetime.

Focusing on health and strength and happiness.
Putting me, myself and my mental state first.
Treating her the same way I would anyone else.
I always see the best in them so I'm well versed.

This time next year I'll be healthy and skinny
and brand new.
On second thought, there might be a bit more
work to do...

Livin' on The Run

I'm not being dramatic,
But it feels like I'm on the run,
Having to do a no jumping, no noise workout,
Just isn't that fun.

I'm not being dramatic,
But a new hotel room every week,
Feels like an overreaction,
We worked from home during the pandemic!

I'm not being dramatic,
If I see another maccies, BK or KFC,
I'm going to throw up,
It'll be 98% salt, you'll see.

I'm not being dramatic,
But I'm not sure these sheets were washed,
Dubious stains on off-white sheets,
Too British to say, my complaint's quashed.

I'm not being dramatic,
I'm just in love with my bed more than anyone,
If I'm in a hotel room again next week,
I think I actually would rather be on the run.

I Will Survive

I will survive this hangover from hell.
My stomach is rolling and it won't quell.
Someone's cooking - is that bacon I smell?
Whoever's making breakfast should be locked in
a cell!

I will survive this headache from Hades.
With a nice warm drink (and a touch of Baileys).
A glasses day for sure - I'll take out my contact
lens dailies.
Close my eyes and dream of quiet jelly babies.

I will survive this period from purgatory.
It might feel like it, but this isn't the end of my
story.
I'm bleeding, but no sympathy, and I'm feeling a
bit predatory.
So I'll snap and snarl and be generally
unsavoury.

I will survive this flu from the fiery depths.
Hacking up a lung, struggling to take deep
breaths.
Lying in bed all day, and slowly losing strengths.

No desire to get up, or to shower, or to take
steps.

I will survive. I will survive unless I don't.
Send soup and ginger and sympathy, because my
family won't.
They say I'm fine and I've misdiagnosed.
But it's not being dramatic if it comes with a
doctor's note!

Friendly Fricative

Forever forgetting to take fabulous photos
Of fake fights, fun-taking and feasting
Of theatre trips, fantastic films and fairs

Drinking dodgy drafts and dad dancing
Disasterously dialling dirtbags
And distressing designated drivers

Reaching for a ready reliable response
Realistically, rarely rapidly replying
Ritually, repeatedly remaining on read

I spy a slippery slithering sibilant snake
Softly swears to select a Spotify song
Since, still stuck on some other sound

I've an inclination to imagine independence
Investigating incidents individually
I inevitably incur imaginary injury

Each and every hour enjoyed emphatically
Entirely excluding everything else
Expressing easily or existing here

Not necessary to be needing more
Nearly never not needing you nearby
Never not nearby when in need

Bad Ideas

24

Do you ever have a great idea?
And by the time you realise it's no good,
It's too late. You try but you can't stop it,
All you can do is hope, pray and touch wood.

A poem based on alliteration
Is a clever idea in theory,
But it leaves you tongue tied and doesn't flow,
And not enough words start with 'i' or 'e'.

Stages of A Run

Stage one begins with the mental warm up,
Telling yourself of course you can do this,
But you're not so sure, then shin splints flare up,
Start to wish you'd warmed up but you digress.

Stage two is the reason that you're still here,
Legs pumping, lungs burning and heart racing,
Wishing you could run through the stratosphere,
Settling for the horizon, chasing.

Stage three, well here's when things start to get
old,
The playlist isn't what it used to be,
If my calves could talk then they'd start to scold,
Maybe running is no longer for me?

Stage four means the finish line is in sight,
A new lease of life and the sprint is on,
Must be the tunnel's end, I see the light,
Gasping, hands on knees, till the bright spot's
gone.

Stage five: ice bath.

Stage six: I really need to find new hobbies.

Squash

What's a type of gourd, that you put into a soup?
Boil it, mash it, and then turn it into goop.
Squash
What do you add water to, to make a kind of
juice?
Or for a bit more fun, put in some Grey Goose.
Squash
What is it called, when you squeeze really really
tight?
Till you can't feel your hands, squeeze with all
your might.
Squash.

What is the best sport to ever have been played?
Played tennis once, but since then I've not
strayed.
Squash
What gets your blood flowing and your heart
racing?
No not that, a little less embracing.
Squash
What uses a ball with two yellow dots?
A racquet, wall, and so many different shots.
Squash

What is now not in the Olympic Games?
An elite sport where no one knows your names.
Squash
Courts disappearing as the funding fails?
Knees getting injured, decreasing court sales.
Squash
What is a sport that messes with your head?
Mostly mind games, where sanity hangs by a
thread.
Squash

What is a sport that is good when it rains?
An indoor sport you can play in hurricanes.
Squash
What is a pastime that can keep you fit?
That you can really excel at if you commit.
Squash
What is the most fun game that you should try?
Bring it up in every chat and be 'that guy'.
Squash

(No but really, it's not just for the posh,
It really is the best in the world, squash
You can play in November with your moustache
Whenever you want to hit something, play
squash!)

Addicted

A picturesque scene,
Fireplace roaring,
Hot chocolate in hand,
Reading by the fire,
Using light it gave.

Or by a window,
In an autumn dream,
Red and yellow leaves,
Helping paint the scene,
Reading about fall.

In a library,
Watched by scorned rejects,
Whose blurb wasn't right,
Maybe for next time,
They watch jealously.

Imagine eyes closed,
Creating new worlds,
Behind my eyelids,
A break in the speech,
Then a new chapter.

Going back ten years,
I'm under bed sheets,
Torch light is shining,
Bed time was long gone,
Reading in the dark.

All stages of life,
Each age and era,
A book can relate,
Maybe a saga,
So I read a lot.

The Destination

I know I'm meant to enjoy the journey,
And mostly I've loved poem creation,
But there's been a lot of long, sleepless nights,
And I'm glad I've reached the destination.

Three weeks, twenty one days, lots of hours,
Spent staring at blank pages and blank screens,
Turning into silly lines, nonsense rhymes,
Trying to force couplets by any means.

Learning more than I thought or expected,
I've a new appreciation for art,
Motivation, courage and strength needed,
To put pen to paper and spill your heart.

I've giggled, screamed, banged my head against walls,
Glared at innocent inanimate things,
Spent hours researching words on Rhyme Zone,
And seen my imagination grow wings.

But I've not slept properly in three weeks,
And the poem hangover's kicking in,
I'll not write another poem again,
Until the next muse strikes and I give in.

9 789357 212267